Comments from Pawprints Writing Club Members and Readers of " How to Write Your Memoirs "

"These prompts make it so easy!"

"It's so rewarding to see our new book, *Stories From The Heart*, (*Vol. 2),* get on the bestseller list at Amazon.com! But just to know that I got to write these stories, and get them out to other people makes me feel very good."

"I thank you, Ina, for helping me see that I really can write!"

"I really wish my grandparents had told me more about their lives before they died …"

Have you been thinking about writing your own stories? Some reasons you might consider plucking those notes from the shoebox and developing them now:

- Because your kids and grandkids will be thrilled to find out more about you.
- Because your life has spanned interesting times, and your adventures and observations of inventions, events and what turned out to be sweeping changes can be fascinating to others, besides your family.
- Because your experiences can help teach others valuable lessons.
- Because writing your recollections will also help you ... the process heals old hurts.
- Finally, because it really isn't nearly as hard as you think. Try it. As Ina says, it's easier than you think, just like …

How to Write Your Memoirs...
Fun Prompts to Make
Writing – and Reading – Your Life Stories a Pleasure!

By Ina Hillebrandt

a PAWPRESS book

Cover design: Carolyn Allen, Carolyn@SunshineByDesign.com

How to Write Your Memoirs was developed through work with Seniors in author Hillebrandt's Grief Lifters *Un*-Workshops,™ and with people of all ages in Idea Magic™ Creativity and Pawprints Writing Clubs.™ For more information on these programs or group sales of our books, please check our website http://www.InasPawprints.com. Books also available through bookstores, Amazon.com and other online distributors. You can also contact publisher Pawpress directly about programs and books. Voice: 310.471.5048. E-mail: annap@InasPawprints.com. Mailing address: Brentwood Village, PO Box 492213, Los Angeles, CA 90049.

How to Write Your Memoirs

Fun Prompts to Make Writing – and Reading – Your Life Stories a Pleasure!

By Ina Hillebrandt

What people are saying about Ina's prompts in "How To Write Your Memoirs"

"I love this *Memoir* book! I've been wanting to write about my parents, and my own life, for my kids ... this is great! Makes it really easy." *Linda B, Beverly Hills, CA*

"The ideas in the *How To Write Your Memoirs* book are really good for the seniors in my writing class. It's helping them feel better ... having writing to look forward to is really important."
Elaine, Director, Senior Center, Prunedale, CA

"Writing is helping me get over the grief I've been carrying around for years."
Jane Madeline, Author, "Stories From The Heart," Vol. 2, by The Pawprints Writing Club

"Looking at these stories other people wrote, I think *I* can do that!"
Sophie Chudacoff, Senior Dynamo, Contributing author, "Stories From the Heart," Vol.2

"Thank you, Ina for helping our Dad get through the pain of losing our Mom, and for bringing us closer. We've been anxious to read the stories he wrote about the family, and surprised to see all his stories about the (fictional) family of Mo the cat. We're glad they are making other people laugh. We had no idea he could write like this!"
Family of Earl Boretz, First-time writer, Pawprints Writing Club, contributing author, "Stories From the Heart," Vols. 1 and 2, InasPawprints.com

"We at the Felicia Mahood Senior Multipurpose Center have the good fortune of being able to offer *Grief Lifters* and *The Pawprints Writing Club* to our seniors. Participants' response to these two excellent workshops has been overwhelmingly positive and appreciative. Ina Hillebrandt is a nationally recognized workshop leader, speaker and author of the Amazon.com top seller *Pawprints*. She has made a positive impact on all of the participants in both workshops. I highly recommend them to anyone who has experienced a loss in their life or who would like to realize their own growth potential in ways they never experienced or thought possible." *Sherrie Berlin, Recreation Coordinator*

"I wholeheartedly recommend Ina Hillebrandt. Her approach to helping seniors ... is unique and brought comfort to all who attended." *Summer Rogers, Program Director, The Park Lane Classic Residence by Hyatt*

"Ina's workshop at The Commonwealth Club really got us to open up and get involved. It's got me thinking in a whole new way." *Edward Buttner, President, Coastcom*

"Ina's work tickles the intellect and creates a new way of seeing ourselves, the world and our place in it." *Tom Beardslee, V.P., Dean Witter*

"Our book (Ina contributed to content and structure) bears witness to her finesse at leading discussion groups, her attentiveness to what individuals wanted to say (and often wouldn't without being prodded), and her rather uncanny awareness of where the group wanted to go...."
Bruce Chapin, author, "The Hardest Challenge," published by TIAA/CREF

"I sing no praise for Georgette or Wilhemina My accolade is for Ina ... She gave my heart a sudden cause With her writing theme of squirrely paws.	"She led the group Just like a maestro And pulled out ideas To flow and flow.	"Did I say she is a real pro? I could go and go On her expertise and skill. How much time do you have to kill?"

Excerpted from a poem by Alan Tichenor, Bishop, CA

About "Stories From The Heart," Vol. 2, Amazon.com bestseller written by the author's Pawprints Writing Club

"These words are alive. The stories are so honest, they're really refreshing! ...'Joey Kowalski was my boyfriend, I think.' (The first sentence in a piece by Jane Madeline.) ... completely charming! And Kay Roberts' line, 'I was born the day they first served beer after the repeal of Prohibition'! It takes me back ... what she says about the Depression, when having children was a luxury, people couldn't afford them ... It was true ... Nobody had any money. It reminds me of our dog Boy, and how he used to go on the bus and come back with food for us. The butcher would wrap up meat and he'd bring it home..."

Geraldine Schlein, former choreographer and businesswoman, lived in Paris with her artist husband in the '20's. Schlein is still active in the arts, an avid reader, pianist and member of the Boards of Robertson Library, the New Music Program of the Los Angeles Philharmonic, UCLA Design for Sharing youth music program

"There's something in here for everyone -- the people are from so many different backgrounds, and their stories are all so entertaining!" *M. Norello, Architect/Designer, Los Angeles*

"This book is so good...the *Pawprints* writing group creates a sense of community, which people lack these days. People get to tell their stories — that's the best thing. And the book is beautiful. With the book, the website where I read some of the stories first, altogether, what a great service!" *Diane Slade, artist and therapist, Napa, California*

About Ina's Amazon.com bestseller "Pawprints," the book that appeared on The Nightly News with Peter Jennings, on PBS in Florida, KCAL TV news, etc.

"This is one of the few books with animal stories I would give as a gift." *Reviewer on Google.com*

"*Pawprints* is filled with enchanting stories I read over and over."
Ann Bennett, housewife, New Jersey

"*Pawprints* is a new form of 'Great Literature,' *Catalytic Literature*. It has the power to change the way people think...The stories are like verbal snapshots...readers feel they are there."
Maxwell Yerger, Reading Teacher/Trainer and Science Teacher

"Dear Ina: I just wanted to say again how much I've enjoyed working with you. *Pawprints* is such a great book – both a wonderful read and an effective teaching tool. When the stories were read aloud in our Educators' Workshop, I felt a warming in the room...Thanks so much for all that you do. Best, Hans," *Hans Cole, Deputy Director, Roots & Shoots, Jane Goodall Institute*

"I was going to read just a story – I'm in the midst of a novel – and I read the whole book. I glanced at it and got enchanted and read it from front to back ... It's so whimsical and charming." *Gratefully, Shirley Oreck*

"*Pawprints* is a potpourri of charming little stories, with a surprise on every page ... vivid observations of life, written from a very different, engaging point of view." *Carol Bruscha, Editor, Los Angles Sierra Club Newsletter*

"Aside from his sister who services those in search of love for hire, his brother who cooked the books at Enron, inflating the number of mice he eliminated, and the two academics that were mistaken for lab animals, Mo has many other colorful siblings."

By Earl Boretz, one of a series of stories called MoTails, invented memoirs of Mo the cat and his relatives, from "Stories From The Heart," Vol. 1

"It was early in 1942, actually Lincoln's birthday, when Mother and Ovie went to Ft. Lauderdale and got married. I not only didn't get to be flower girl, I didn't even get to be there. I was having tomato soup with Malcolm and his mother."

By Kay Roberts, from "Where Do We go from Here?" ... a work in progress in "Stories From The Heart," Vol. 2, Amazon.com bestseller with cover art by Carolyn Allen, Illustrations by Jane Madeline and Andre Van Zijl
Edited, and designed by Ina Hillebrandt, published by Pawpress

"His remains fall from the sky. Gray billowing wings dust the bleating rumps of seven gemsbok, galloping below. John and I lean back as the twin engine Cessna banks left over a sliver of gilded horizon. Sunset flares in the distance with fat summer cumuli emptying their bellies over the Kalahari Desert. We sigh with relief, we have fulfilled our father's last request: his pagan wish to have his ashes spread over the hunting grounds of his youth. Images of his brick red face and the enveloping calm of his seemingly Titan presence engulfs us as we sit back into the folding night, children again."

By Andre Van Zijl, from "A Country Not Made By Men," excerpted in "Stories From The Heart," Vol. 2

"My son promised he'd do it. But he's 16, and you know how *that* goes. So, one day I just went in there and said, 'O.K., snake. You don't like me, and I don't like you, but I have to clean your cage...' Next thing I know, he was gone. I looked everywhere, the bathtub, under the bed. Finally I opened the closet door, and there were two beady eyes, staring out at me..."

From "Snake Eyes," a first story in the life of Miss B., bilingual childcare provider at Pawprints Writers Workshop

Preface

How to Write Your Memoirs has grown out of workshops I've been leading, for more years than I care to admit, with people from the corporate world, the world of wellness, and most recently, Pawprints™ literacy and creative writing programs for kids and seniors.*

It contains organizing ideas, prompts and reminiscences from both my own and students' lives. Use these to jump-start your own creative juices. You'll see your musings will range from spicy, zestful and smile-inducing to calm, informative, and believe it or not, un-boring!

Is there a philosophy underlying the prompts and the whole process? Absolutely! We all need to lighten up! If my work has shown me anything, it's that many of us fear we cannot write anything, or be creative, for a whole variety of reasons. It's also shown me that not taking ourselves too seriously coaxes our creative genies out of their bottles. Consequently, from time to time you might find a little surprise in the pages that follow; I'm sure you'll find many in your own memory banks.

So go ahead. Use the tips and examples in the pages of this book, and banish those "I'm not creative" and "I can't write" monsters from your vocabulary. I'll bet once you start jotting down your recollections, you'll have a hard time stopping!

In fact, you may wind up joining me in the Computer Cooking Club.™ That's the one that features my special breakfast recipe:

Ina's Magic Egg

Take a small pot, just big enough for one egg
Put egg into pot
Add cold water to cover
Add ½ tsp salt to keep eggshell from cracking
Turn on heat to high
Go back to computer, resuming project
When you hear the explosion, the egg is done.

Happy tails!

Ina

* For information on Pawprints Literacy Plus™ and the Pawprints Writing Clubs™ creative writing programs, please check our website at http://www.InasPawprints.com.

Otters and a Sea Lion

Photo © Ina Hillebrandt

Near the Monterey, California Aquarium and Fishing Pier

Table of Contents

Photo courtesy of Pawprints Writing Club author, Kay Roberts, originally published in "Stories From The Heart, Vol. 2"

Introduction
Why bother? Who Cares?

Why write your memoirs? This may seem to be a simple-minded question, but I am posing it seriously because of a 92-year-old lady I've worked with who's become a friend. She keeps saying she wants to write, and what she wants to write is profiles of her grandkids. My response, "That would be wonderful, but how about starting with your own story? I feel sure that your kids and grandkids would treasure your stories. Writing down your adventures, experiences, feelings and observations would be a great gift to them. They'd love to know about the kinds of things that happened in your life, and how you felt about things."

"You know," she answered me, "I have had an interesting life. I've been very lucky in the men I was married to. We really had a lot of fun." (She has been married and widowed three times, and speaks highly of all three men. As do their families about her – a rich gift indeed to share.) She also talked about the travel she's enjoyed, the work she's done (and is still doing), and the myriad activities she enjoys to this day. This is a lady who has been instrumental in helping a major medical institution raise millions of dollars, and she is still president of the chapter she helped found, now almost in its fiftieth year. Though she honestly feels the group would benefit by having a new person with new ideas, "They won't let me quit, honey," she tells me. And it's true – I've seen them, and her, in action. I wouldn't let her quit either. She's quite an inspiration. Imagine how useful her insights and practical ideas on how to raise funds for worthwhile causes would be to others, just for one example, and how interesting all these experiences, and her more personal ones, would be to her family.

Another reason I say your story is valuable is its potential for healing. Comments from children of a man who attended my workshops on grief and writing pointed this up. They have been amazed to read his stories showing how much he loved his wife, and how much he grieved over her after she died. He'd been the kind to keep emotions rather hidden, and they just did not know how deeply he felt about her. This made them feel much better about her life, as they had some concerns that he hadn't loved her enough. His writings also helped bring him to the point where he could talk with the kids in ways he hadn't before; the whole process began a form of communication and family healing none of them expected.

What's really odd – but then as some of us feel, there are no coincidences – is that my own memories are being piqued now. Because of the miracle of the web, a relative from my father's side of the family has contacted my daughter, and then me, wanting to share her knowledge and also to find out more about our family history from our vantage point. The notes flying back and forth between the two of us are really fulfilling. She and I are finding out more about our past, our history, and our futures, too, as we share stories about our children.

But it's the stories of our parents that we're both focused on at the moment – the longing to know more about what their lives were like before we came into being, what shaped them. And how their skills, habits, traits affected us, and in turn, our children.

In a nutshell, here are some of the reasons you might consider taking time out to sit down and inscribe your memories:

- Because your kids and grandkids will be thrilled to find out more about you.

- Because your life has spanned interesting times, and your adventures and observations of inventions, events and what turned out to be sweeping changes can be fascinating to others, besides your family.

- Because your experiences can help teach others valuable lessons.

- Because finding out about former times is fun for those who didn't personally experience them, and fun to relive!

- Because finding out another's viewpoint of former times is fun for those who did live through them, too, plus – your recollections will stimulate other people to compare notes with you. They'll embark on their own mental journeys of reminiscence with your help.

- Because writing about your recollections will also help you. No matter what great realizations and growth we've had in our lives, there are always events and people lurking in the recesses of our minds, waiting to pop out and either enlighten or scare us. But getting them out, into the light, is the ultimate healer. Facing them, good or bad, is illuminating and rejuvenating. Memories can bring a great deal of joy to us. Those that are difficult can lead us to closure finally. Once we allow them to come out of the closet, they just plain lose their power over us.

- Finally, because it really isn't nearly as hard as you think. The key is simple, really ... just give yourself permission to try. What have you got to lose?

- BECAUSE FAMILY STORIES SHOULDN'T BE FORGOTTEN BUT PASSED ON FROM GENERATION TO GENERATION
  - SCHOOL ASSIGNMENTS
  - KNOWING SOMETHING ABOUT YOUR ANCESTORS MAY HELP YOU KNOW YOURSELF
  - SEE THAT YOU AREN'T ALONE. PARENTS & GP FACED SAME PROBLEMS YOU DO

So where do I start? Shaping your Memoirs

There are probably as many ways to go about organizing your thoughts as there are people. One way is simply to make up your mind to begin! Then sit down and just let whatever comes to mind bubble up, and jot it down (or type it into the computer). That's really my favorite beginning.

Another idea is to think of someone you know, and imagine you are telling that person a story out loud. Just start writing as if you were speaking with him or her.

Once words start to flow, you might find that your memories could be channeled into chapters. Again, there are different ways you might want to think about putting those together. Here are some ideas to consider:

- Chronologically, and/or by decade
- By outside events, such as world-changing cataclysms or marvels
- By family events
- By romances
- By adventures
- By travels
- By hobbies
- By jobs
- By happiest moments
- By scariest moments
- By triumphs
- By failures/learning experiences
- By things you'd like younger people to know
- By things you'd like your family to know

You could, of course, start by willing up memories in the categories above, or others of your own.

Since the chronological approach is the one that makes the best sense to most of us, this book is focused on taking you through the path of early to grownup years.

You'll find cues or prompts to spark recall beginning with your earliest memories, recollections of your family, hometown, school days, and then your own years as a grownup, recapping feelings, your own traditions, and children if you have them. You'll also find prompts for looking back over time, both from the perspective of outside events and personal reflections. Many of the categories outlined on the previous page are included, but you might want to add any that are not (such as "scariest moments") to help you form a coherent story that suits you best. The Table of Contents, pages 3 and 4, has an outline of all prompt categories, and you can start with the first, and go in order, or jump around as things come to you.

You'll see only one prompt on some pages. This is to help you focus, if you like, on just one thought at a time. You can even copy these pages and write directly below the idea as an alternate way of engaging your creative spirit!

Whatever you do, I hope you'll view the prompts and reminiscences as a way to trigger your own memory. By absolutely no means should you feel that you have to incorporate them all to make your own writing complete. Rather, use the materials and stories as gentle muses, there to stimulate recall, as you craft your own personal, and appealing memoirs.

Above all, have fun! Put on music you like, set up a comfortable writing area. If you're writing in longhand, pick pens or pencils that flow easily, and for extra fun, use colors!

Note: Pictures Are Worth A Thousand Words, No?

Do you have any pictures of you as you were growing up? Of family, friends, pets? If so, you may find it wonderful fun, and stimulating, to take them out and look at them as you are responding to the cues or prompts in these pages.

You could also get copies made and incorporate them into the book you are going to create!

Here are a couple of tips on how to include pictures.

First, if you are not using a computer, you can take any color or black and white photo to a one-hour photo shop, or to a self-service machine that duplicates photos, or to a copy shop such as Kinko's, and paste your copy where you would like it to illustrate what you are writing about.

For those of you who have computers, if you have a scanner, I recommend scanning the photos at the highest resolution you can. You can then crop and resize your photos, and export them to a folder you can easily find. I recommend you save your pictures in a .tiff format if you are a PC user, as this prepares a loss-less resolution quality, and the best for print. (When sending pictures over the web, you want to use a jpg or gif format, which create much smaller files for easy transmission, but are not as good for printing.) When you export/save your photos, use a dpi of at least 300 and you can print a very good image to place where you want with your text. (You Mac users know more than I do about graphics, so go to it!)

For computer users without scanners, you can go to a Kinko-type shop and pay them for scans. Or ask the kids and grandkids, of course!

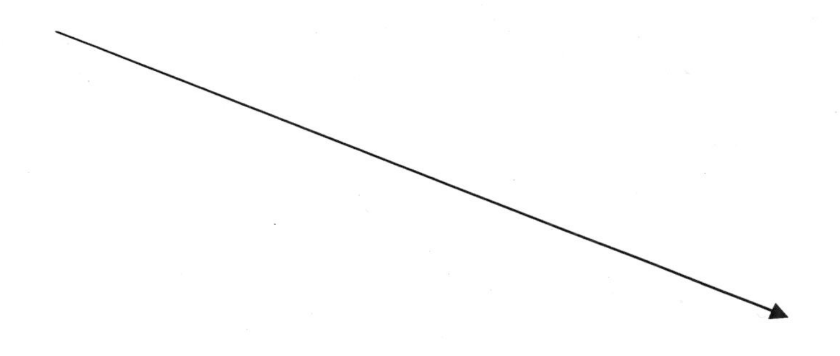

Memoir Writing Prompts and Samples

My very first memory as a kid is of my aunt, bending down behind me, hands on my shoulders, telling me to say, "Hubba, hubba!" when my Dad came through the door. This was on the day he returned from World War II. My Mom was behind us, standing on the curved stairway, also facing the door.

I don't have a lot of details of the scene, but I remember this much vividly. I was three years old.

Another early memory of mine comes from a short time later. My parents decided to move us away from Philadelphia, and out to California. My Dad's sister lived there, and it sounded like the right place to be to him. The Aunt, Aunt Soph, was in Philadelphia visiting, and joined us for the drive back to LA. What I remember so well is being frightened to death on the top of very steep mountains. My Dad had to turn around at one point, having made a mistake apparently. My aunt was so afraid we'd go over the edge that she wouldn't stay in the car while he made the U-turn. It's amazing I'm not scared of heights today. My first horseback ride, at age 13, was on the top of a very narrow, steep cliff. I wasn't afraid for a second; just was completely exhilarated by being up on a horse.

In the Beginning ...

- Think back to the time you were a kid.
- What is the very first thing you can remember?
- Was this a person?
- Who was it?
- A parent, other relative?
- What did the person look like?
- What other things do you remember about him/her?
- What was happening?
- What was your interaction with the person?
- Was it fun? Not fun?
- What were your feelings? Where were you?
- What was around you – describe the scene as best you can. Any sounds? Any smells?

My father said his very first memory was of being able to see over the dining room table. Me, I remember seeing the tips of cat's tails over the dining room table, later in life, but I don't remember the same landmark from my own kidhood. Do you? Any other milestones come to mind?

.....

Alternate Beginning ...

- What's the very first memory that comes to your mind?
- How old are you in this scene?
- What's going on?
- Who are you with, if anyone?
- Where are you?
- What's happening?
- What can you see around you? What can you hear? Feel? Smell?

Remember any books you read as a kid? Any animals you saw?

And Going On From The First Questions ...

- Was this (first childhood memory) a special event?
    - Was it more of an everyday thing?
- What was your event or everyday occurrence?
- Where was it?
- What was going on?
- Were there other people there?
- Animals?
- Was it outdoors? Indoors?
- Do you remember colors, in addition to sounds, smells?
- What feelings come up when you think back to this event?

The piece below comes from Earl Boretz, a man who said of himself, "I can't write" before becoming one of the most prolific and entertaining writers in the Pawprints Writing Club™ in Los Angeles. Another sibling story of Earl's, of a totally different nature, follows on page 15.

MEMORIES

By Earl Boretz

My sister made me feel good when I was with her. She was very down-to-earth, and I had no trouble understanding her; there was no confusion. Her personality was vibrant, alive and animated, and those traits became mine when I was with her.

Despite my feelings for her, I always felt cheated because she had a sister but I had no brother. One day she met a wonderful guy and they married. Lo and behold, I had a loving, caring big brother. There was nothing this guy couldn't or wouldn't do for me. He got me my first car. And in 1946, I saw a cartoon, "Motor Mania." In that cartoon, Goofy has a car with a gun sight to aim at pedestrians. I really wanted a sight like that on my car. Not only did he get it for me, he put it on the car so it couldn't be stolen. Everybody noticed my car.

All my life I wanted an electric train, but my parents thought I was too young. He got me an electric train with extra track, and two bridges that lit up.

The love and respect I had for him I have today. He is the only person I feel indebted to, to this day. He lives in northern San Diego, and we still visit and talk, and if I need anything he's like Santa Claus. He and my sister are two of the best memories in my life.

Our Family Members When We Were Kids
Brothers and Sisters

*N*ote: Sometimes people would rather tackle recollections of siblings before parents, which is why this section is first. But if your mind goes to stories about your parents first, turn to the next section and jump in!

- Do/did you have brothers/sisters?

- Describe one of your siblings –

  - Physical appearance – hair, eye color, body type, height
  - Types of clothes he/she likes/liked to wear
  - Favorite sayings
  - Favorite music
  - Favorite activities

Just for fun – this is a fanciful tale spun by Earl. You can find many more tales of his cat Mo's imaginary family on our website http://www.InasPawprints.com. A book containing all Earl's stories, real and invented, will soon be available through our site as well. Look for Tales from the Heart at our online store.

MoTails #2
THE CANDIDATE
By Earl Boretz

There are those rare occasions when a window of opportunity opens for a short time. So it is with Mo. Like Arnold Schwarzenegger, he, too, is on the Governor's recall ballot. The reality of this election is it doesn't take a lot of votes to get elected. So Mo decided to throw his litter box into the race and get his fifteen minutes of fame. However, unlike Arnold, Mo has expressed definite issues. Which he'll be unveiling for the electorate to ponder after the debates.

Last week, Mo's sister decided to bask in her brother's glory. She invited him to a fundraiser at a popular nightclub. Mo hadn't seen his sister for a long period of time, but wasn't going to turn down any financial assistance. Though he had second thoughts about the offer, the time and date were set. That's all Mo had to know. He figured, what did he have to lose.

He arrived early, and almost immediately had a bad feeling in the pit of his stomach. When he met his sister, her dress and make-up left nothing to the imagination as to her profession. She gave him her card; she ran a cathouse. In short order his sister's employees appeared. There was little doubt as to how she would fill his coffers. Mo was flabbergasted. But those invited to contribute were willing to make the sacrifice.

When the festivities concluded, Mo let his sis know in no uncertain terms this was the end of their relationship. His final words to her were, "Hasta la vista, Baby!" Mo really got mad at his sister in that nightclub.

- What were your brother(s)'/sister(s)' attitudes:

  - Toward the world
  - Toward your parents
  - Toward you
  - Toward school
  - Toward life as a kid
  - Toward life as a grownup

- Did these (attitudes) change over time? How would you say your brother/sister feels about these things today? Is this different from "kid hood" days?

- Did you get along with your brother(s)/sister(s) when you were kids?
- Describe a good day between/among you as kids.
- Describe a bad day between/among you as kids.

- What kinds of things did/do you do together?
- Did you fight over chores?

- Did you ever put on a show? Go swimming? Skate? Ride bikes? Roller skate? Go to the movies together? What other things did you do together?

- How do you feel about your relationship with your sibs overall?

    - What are the best things about it?

    - Any things you'd like to be different?

    - Is there anything you can do now to alter how your relationship is? (Hint: Sometimes we harbor regrets and a person may no longer be alive. But I have learned that we can communicate in a way by writing to that person, or by speaking to someone else, someone we trust.)

- After going through the exercises for one sibling, do the same for other(s) you may have.

Our Parents

- Describe your parents in the same way as you did your siblings.
- Add whatever other emotions, memories are appropriate.
- Did you listen when they told you what to do?
- Did you agree with them?
- When you didn't, what happened?

- Where did your mother come from?
- Was she born in the US?
- Where?
- What was her early life like in that town/city?

- Ditto for your father – where was he born? In the US?
- What was his childhood like – what do you know or remember about stories you've heard about it?

- Were your parents born outside the US?
- Where?
- Why did they come to the US?
- Were they glad they did?
- What were some of the differences when they got here, if they remembered? What were some of their earliest memories of their trip here, of their first sight of the country? Of first few months here?

- What are some of the best things your Mom ever taught you?

- What are some of the best things your Dad ever taught you?
- If you were brought up by someone other than Mom and Dad, did the people bringing you up teach you some "best things"?

- What is the thing that makes you saddest about your parents, or the people who brought you up?
- Happiest about them?
- What's the best thing you ever did for them?
- The worst? Have you forgiven yourself yet?

- Think back to some event your parents took you to.
- What was it?
- Did you have a good time?
- What was the best thing about it?
- Would you do it again, if you could?

- Is it something you could do for your own children, if you have, or plan to have kids?
- Have you already shared this with them?
- How close to what you remember as a kid was the experience for you?
- For them?

- Are your parents still living? If so, do you see them? Often? What's the best thing about that?

- If they are not still living, do you still communicate in some way (many do, and it can be a comfort – see below).

- Is there something you have never been able to say to them that you would like to? Try writing a letter to them. See how that makes you feel.

Our Own Early Days ... Our Home Towns

- Where were you born?
- In what town?
- What was it like back then?

Us kids always found something to do at Victor Street. The house was a two story New Jersey home with siding, steps and cement. In the upstairs was the apartment where my friends' grandmother lived. She was Mr. Jorgensen's mother. Mrs. Jorgensen's mother lived in her own house near the Passaic River. Let me say since I had no aunts and uncles I was always told to call Mr. and Mrs. Jorgensen 'Aunt Betty' and 'Uncle Roy.' In fact, all us kids called them that...One of the best times I remember was the time us kids tried to distill our own wine – 'The Great Grape Fiasco.'

By Jane Madeline, from "The Great Grape Fiasco," in "Stories From The Heart," Vol. 2

- Is it different now?
- Do you still live there?
- If not, if you were to go back now, what would you expect to see?
- Would the shops be the same?
- The houses?
- Streets?
- Schools?
- Parks?
- Playgrounds?
- Statues?
- People?
- Newspaper?
- Local radio station(s), if your town had one or more?
- Can you remember some of the big local news stories when you were growing up?
- Can you remember a local hero? What was the story?
- Was there a local bad guy? What happened?
- Did people visit each other's homes often? Was that fun? Is that still true, in your life?
- Were there chili bake-offs? Who was known for the best chili in town?
- Were there barbecues? Where were they? Who tended the grill?

After Our Hometown, If We Became Rolling Stones Or Even Moved Just Once As Kids …

- If you moved from your hometown, where did you move?
- What was that place like?
- How was it the same/different from your hometown?
- Were the people different?
  - In the way they dressed, behaved?
  - How would you describe these differences?
- Were traditions different?
- Were the looks of the town different? How?
  - Did you move from a small town to a large city?
  - How did the new place strike you – was it overwhelming? Inviting? Exciting? Scary? Fun?
  - Did you do the reverse, and move from a large city to a smaller one? How did the smaller town pace, people, style affect you?
- Were the same kinds of things to do available? (Sports, movies, dances, social events, clubs, other activities?)
- Were there things you missed when you left your hometown? What were they?
- Were there people you missed? Did you stay in touch? How did you do that? How might that be different today, with all the communication tools at our fingertips? Would people stay closer to each other?
- Were there things that made you thrilled you'd left? What were they?

Home for Faeries Designed by John Crawford and available through http://www.fairywoodland.com

Look anything like the homes in your old neighborhood?

Prompts for Early Years, Whether in Our Home Town or Other Roost(s)

- What were some of the regular events that happened when you were growing up?
- Were they fun?
- What sorts of events were they?
- Were there fairs?
- Were there spring celebrations?
- Were there harvest festivals?
- Did people gather to go Christmas Caroling?
- Who participated?
- Who didn't (were they scoffers?)?

We grew up in a Jewish home, but my parents were not very religious. Every year my brother and I got the best of both worlds. We got to celebrate the eight days of Chanukah, with presents and candles all eight days, plus we also got a Christmas tree and a Christmas present. At least until our cat started knocking all the glass ornaments down, shattering them and making for dicey walking for him and for all of us.

Then there were many other holidays, of course. I can remember the interminable wait until we could eat at Seders at my grandparents' house in Philadelphia. My grandfather, who really was not religious, somehow found it important to go through the entire Haggadah, book of all the Seder prayers and rituals, preceding the first bite of food, or at least meaningful bite. What kid likes horseradish, after all? But there were lots of us gathered around the table, and that was fun, and my grandmother, my Mom's mother, was a magnificent cook. So when we finally did get to eat, we feasted. Afterward, we got to look for the money that had been hidden, all of us kids hoping we would be the one to find it. The entire cast of characters, at least twenty of us, had a great time at these dinners.

My grandmother, I also remember, was forever saying about her cooking, "I made a mistake! Don't eat this!" and I was forever saying, "Gram, I'll eat your mistakes any time!" This little lady, with the most luxurious wavy silver hair, had the lightest touch imaginable in the kitchen. Her piecrusts were perfect. Her knishes took three days to prepare. She would roll out the dough on the kitchen table, as thin as paper, and make a gazillion little morsels so all of us could have trays to take home. I especially loved the potato knishes, with rice a distant second. Liver you could feed to the pussycat as far as I was concerned. Unfortunately, I never learned the knish recipe, but I can make her wonderful tomato soup and stewed tomatoes, and sugar cookies. And I can also prepare my Mom's scalloped potatoes and broiled chicken, two of her best dishes, and long favorites of mine.

Excuse me. I'm getting hungry. I think I'll go boil an egg.

Holidays Bring Up Lots of Stuff – the Good, the Bad, the Ugly – and the Wondrous

- What happened on holidays when you were growing up?
- Take one holiday and describe how your family celebrated it.
- Then describe another.
- You might want to go through the years and compare how those holidays hit you now versus how they hit you when you were a kid.

As a grownup, I decided to incorporate both the Jewish and Christian spirit of my own early days into my own annual party in New York. I'd invite gangs of clients, friends and family, and we'd all mingle happily drinking my homemade eggnog and eating the chestnuts I'd roast, and cookies I'd baked. After a couple of hours, I'd find a person who really knew the Jewish story of Chanukah, and everyone would gather round as he or she told it. Then we'd go back to mingling and noshing. After about an hour, when I felt sufficient time had passed for that story to sink in, we moved to the Christmas tree. I'd asked everyone to bring a homemade ornament. Anyone who hadn't was asked to dig in to the supplies I had on hand and create something. That tree was full of love, and fun, every year!

I remember my husband's family's Christmastime, in Lake Charles, Louisiana. The whole town was alive with the most positive spirit of the holiday. Whenever you entered anyone's home, you felt as if you were jumping into a warm bath. The hospitality was genuine, and very welcome to me. I'd spent my childhood in big cities, and half in the north. Not that folks were cold, but it was a different sort of welcome, more restrained. In Lake Charles, as soon as you came in the door, people gathered around, offered you something to eat and drink, and the warmth just oozed from the sofa cushions.

I started to ooze myself, or at least grow, as things like "Nuts and Bolts" were put in front of me. An artery-clogging snack made of Chex cereal, peanuts, pretzels and other salty snacks I'm probably forgetting, this mixture was soaked in bacon fat and slow-roasted. It was absolutely delicious, and it was impossible to eat less than whatever was put in front of you.

- Do you have any memories like these from when you were growing up? How would you describe your times at holidays?
- Which ones did you especially enjoy? Have you kept any of these going as a grownup?
- Were there family traditions when you were growing up?

In sixth grade, in Philadelphia, we had foreign languages one semester, and were introduced to Latin and French. Our teacher was a Parisian-born older woman, with a white-powdered face, shaved, penciled eyebrows, bright round spots of rouge on her cheeks, permanently pursed red-painted lips, and a weird shade of red-dyed hair. She had retained a perfect French accent, and I've considered myself blessed to have heard the proper way to pronounce the language. I studied French later for a number of years, and when I speak slowly, or when I've had a little wine and stop being self-conscious, my accent is pretty fair, a holdover from those days, I've always felt.

I remember being taught how to write checks in one class, how to sew in another, and how to cook, how to climb ropes, march and play volley ball in those awful pantaloon gym suits we girls had to wear. I remember we used to bunch up the extra fabric and tuck it under the pants, so we wouldn't look so huge. About the rope climbing, I remember having no arm strength and pulling myself up with my legs. I remember the "horse," a tan, stationary, leather-covered imitation we had to jump up on. I remember dance classes, and loving them. I remember "Point your little footie," the waltz, rumba, cha cha, fox trot, tango, and later the jitterbug and swing, but the last two were not from school.

In cooking class, I remember one day I was in charge of hot chocolate, which I loved. The batch I made was awful – so bitter it almost hurt your mouth. Turned out I'd forgotten the sugar. But I was always proud of myself for admitting it, and then we could correct the mistake. Not always so easy I've seen as a grownup.

I remember writing back then for the school magazine, 'The Phalarope.' This was all in Carnel Elementary School, in Philadelphia. I used to concoct adventure stories of the mascot I'd brought to life. The only tale I vaguely remember is the time he found himself in the middle of a bullring in Spain, sitting between the horns of the bull, during a fight. I don't remember how I got him out of that one, but the stories were kind of cliffhangers I think. Which reminds me of the movies on Saturday I used to attend back in LA, with my little brother Conrad. But those are another story.

Elementary School Years

- What memories do you have of your early years in school?
- What kind of school did you attend? Public? Religious? Were you home-schooled?
- How big was your elementary school?
- Do you remember any of your teachers from that time, or later years in school?
- Be as specific as you can – name, appearance, class they taught, special trademark tricks they used to teach you, distinctive traits to their behavior?
- Do you remember any of the subjects you studied, and how you felt about them?

I have lots of memories of those days. I remember Mr. Malone, an English teacher we loved and tortured, but he understood the torture was born of affection. He taught us punctuation one day, I remember, by first drawing a circle on the blackboard. Then he spun around quickly and asked the class, "Isn't that a great circle?" We all applauded, and he bowed. Then he drew another. Another round of applause, and another bow. Finally he drew a third circle for a final burst of applause. The circles were lined up vertically. He told us to think of a traffic signal, with green, yellow and red lights. Then he proceeded to tell us that each color represented a particular punctuation mark, the red being a period – full stop, end of thought, the yellow a comma - pause, the green no stop, full speed ahead (I think). One day, he was late for class, which was very unusual. I conspired with the others to turn our book covers upside down, though the books inside were right side up. We were all busily reading our apparently upside down texts when he came in. He looked around, told us to turn our books around, so that of course they were upside down for real, and called on some of us to read aloud.

I remember Mr. Raspanti, another English teacher. Very dapper, Italian-born. A bit more formal than Mr. Malone, but an equally fine teacher. And I remember a history teacher I absolutely adored, because he allowed us to write in pencil. This meant if we made a mistake, we could erase it. In other classes, we had to use ink. Mistakes meant messes or rewriting the entire page. Our history teacher also allowed us great leeway in using our imaginations. We had a report due for American History, which was our focus that term. It was to be illustrated, and he cautioned, "The pictures must fit what you're writing about," and the "captions have to relate to the text." Being lazy, I'd waited until the night before the report was due. Then I sort of frantically thumbed through magazines we had in the house, a bit desperate to find something, anything! Eureka! A dinosaur. "There were no dinosaurs living in North America at this time," I wrote under the drawing. He gave me an A. I've always loved him for that.

Middle School Years

- What do you remember about middle school?
- Did you start to date in junior high or middle school? What was that like?
- Did you start to do other new things in middle school? What were they?
- What kinds of classes did you have? What years were you in middle school? Grades 6-9? Or were your schools combining classes in different mixes?
- Did you have special holiday celebrations in middle school?
- Did you have elections? Do you remember anyone who was a class president or other officer? Did you ever run? Did you win? What was your campaign based on?
- Did you belong to any clubs? What were they? Why'd you join? Was it fun? What was the best thing about being in them? Anything bad? What was that?
- Did you ever get in trouble in school? What happened? What did your parents do about it? Were you punished? What were punishments in your home?
- Do you remember any class clowns? What can you say about them?
- Remember any class bullies? Ditto.
- Remember any "brains"? Another ditto.
- What was the most fun thing that ever happened in middle school?
- What was the worst thing that happened?
- Do you remember having best friends? What were they like? Did they have weird habits? Fun habits? Sayings? What kinds of clothes did they wear? What did you like to do together?
- Did you have sleepovers? Describe one.
- Did you go camping, with family? With friends, too?

Any of these critters frequent your camp?

Bat pic © AnimationFactory.com, a neat place to visit to get illustrations that enliven your own work, especially if you want to create something your family can access through the web.

Camp

- Did you go to camp? Sleepover? Day camp? What happened? What was the best part of camp? The worst? How was the food? Did you put on a play? What sports did the camp have? Activities? Was it fun?

- Did you put your own kids in camp? What was that like, if you did? Were you ever homesick? Were your kids?

We were very lucky. We had a teacher who read us "The Iliad," and "Beowulf" while walking around the room, in the aisles between our chairs. He was very dramatic, and a lot of fun. I remember his posture. Stomach protruding, eyes cast down on the book as he paced about. He would often pause for effect, sweeping the room with his eyes, making sure we were paying attention. He also gave us creative writing assignments every week. We were all college-bound, and the Honor Class. Rather than let us be full of ourselves, and write pretentiously, he'd command, "No big words!" The format was quite brief, and taught me a style that came to fruition in my book "Pawprints," where no story is more than two pages, and most are one. Lest you think that's simple, remember the adage, "Sorry this is so long. I'd have written less, but I didn't have time."

We had a physics teacher in high school who was pretty clumsy, or just absent-minded; we kids weren't sure which. One day, he bent down to get something from behind a table top to demonstrate some phenomenon or another to us, and when he re-emerged, he'd cut his tie in half, without realizing it. He also habitually wore white shirts with deep perspiration stains under the arms. Many years later, I was sort of ashamed that we made fun of him in a skit the year we had his class.

High School

- OK, did you have grade 10 a and 10 b, the way we did when I was a kid? What do you remember from 10th grade?
- What classes did you have in high school? Which, if any, were fun?
- Were there any you hated? Which, and why?
- What were the most useful? Least useful?
- Did you have a prom? Did you go? What did you wear? Who was the Queen? King? Did they deserve it?
- Have you been to any high school reunions? What has that been like? See any old chums? Have they changed? A lot? A little? Who's still saying the same things, using the same phrases? Who still has hair?
- What was "in" when you were in high school?
- What would teens think of those things today?
- Who were your friends? Are you still in touch?
- What's the thing you miss most about that time in your life?
- What do you miss least?
- If you were in high school today, how would it be different?
- Can people recognize you from your high school yearbook pictures?
- Sometimes there were, especially in years gone by, many circumstances mitigating against people finishing school. If you didn't attend or complete high school, do you feel that's a big loss? Would your life have been different if you'd been able to finish? What would advise kids and parents today about completing high school?

Growing Up

- What's the most amazing thing that ever happened to you as you were growing up?

- What was the most fun thing that ever happened as you were growing up?
- What's the most embarrassing thing that ever happened as you were growing up?

WHAT A RELIEF!

By Earl Boretz

If ever someone was made to be a mother, that person was Ilene. And if one could describe Ilene's concept of Hell it would be the need to drive somewhere. As I said in the past, we are opposites, and next to being different sexes the way we drive is our biggest difference.

Ilene is polite, considerate, and a stickler for obeying the law. She would get in the right turn lane, be confronted by a red light and wait until it turned green. The poor people behind her had to wait for her to make her right. She's the kind of person who could be stopped by a broken red light. She would wait there until someone came to turn it green. I, on the other hand, am very impatient.

One day out of the goodness of her heart, she agreed to drive our son to UCLA; his car had broken down. I stayed home alone, and was enjoying my peace and quiet when the phone rang. It was Ilene, in tears. She'd made a wrong turn and was calling from the Valley. She needed directions on how to get home. I spent the next five minutes trying to convince her I could come to her, but she insisted if she had directions she could make it back. There was one minor condition – she wasn't going on the freeway.

I gave her directions, and decided to sit down and worry for the next ten hours or so, as Ilene doesn't drive fast and stops for everything. An ant line crossing the road could bog her down for hours.

Well, she finally made it home. The look on her face was that of someone who'd won the Super Lotto.

Although she never knew it, I hadn't been that relieved since I saw her at our wedding. I thought with her intelligence she wouldn't show up.

Note: Another story by the man who said he couldn't write, and whose stories brought revelations and healing for his family.

I do . . .

- Are you now, or have you been married?
- How did you and your husband or wife first meet? (For those with more than one marriage, you might want to tell the story of each circumstance.)
- Where were you?
- Did someone introduce you?
- What happened?
- How long was it before you knew you were going to be married?
- What happened during the courtship?
    - Was there one?
    - What one moment stands out as hilarious?
    - What one moment stands out as the most romantic ever?
    - Are there special songs you connect with your courting days?
    - Do you still listen to these?
- What kind of wedding did you have?
    - Was it a civil ceremony?
    - A religious ceremony?
    - Where was it?
    - Who made the arrangements?
    - Were there fights over the plans?
    - How was the ceremony itself? What one part stands out in your mind?
- Where did you go on your honeymoon?
    - How did you choose this place?
    - Was it a good idea to go there?
    - What was the most fun thing you remember from your honeymoon? (Yes, it's OK to be bawdy.)
    - Did anything absolutely horrendous happen?
    - Did your luggage get there on time?
    - Did you ever return to the spot?

THE SIGHTS AND SOUNDS OF A JAPANESE GARDEN
By Bill Safier

You are seated next to your beloved one, holding hands.
You look around and you are surrounded by
beautiful trees, plants and flowers.
The air is filled with the scent of perfume.
Looking out, you see a small waterfall.
Listen carefully, and you will hear a melody played
as the water rushes over the rocks on its journey.

Look up and you see a bird flying, and it's singing its love song to both of
you, as it slowly disappears in the blue sky.

Listen as the garden plays music soft and gentle.
The trees gently sway as if dancing,
as a gentle breeze rustles through the leaves.
You turn towards each other. Your eyes meet, and you both smile.
Slowly, slowly your lips meet, so soft and tender.
Then you speak the most beautiful words in the world, "I love you so much."
Your life has risen to a level whereby God and Love are supreme.

Note: By Bill Safier, a consummate pianist, in our Grief Lifters and Pawprints Writing Workshops in Los Angeles.

- What is the best thing about your marriage (so far)?
- What's the thing that bugs you the most?
- What bugs your spouse the most?
- How would you advise younger married folks?
- What's most important in a good marriage, from your point of view?

Other Romances

- What about other romances in your life? What do you remember about your very first boyfriend or girlfriend? How old were you? How old was he/she? Where was this? Were you in school? Did your parents approve? What kinds of things did you do together? What interested you in him/her? What did he/she look like?

- Do other romantic relationships come to mind? How would you describe your feelings? The people?

Our Own Kids

- Do you have children?
- If so, how many?
- Boy(s)? Girl (s)?
- How old were you when they were born?

My ob-gyns worked as part of a two-man team. This was a terrific concept. The docs alternated seeing you on your routine checkups, so that you would get to know them both, and they would get to know you. Then, when you gave birth, whoever was on call would be up to speed, and you would feel comfortable.

As it turned out, the older of the two on my team did the intake interview. This man must have been at least 70 years old at the time, and heaven knew how many babies he'd delivered. Yet, he put his feet up on his desk, turned in his chair, and for a full 15 minutes waxed philosophical on the absolute wonder of the whole process of pregnancy and birth. I was so moved, and also quite impressed. He was truly a dedicated man.

My husband Barry and I went out immediately and bought a book with pictures of what happens at each stage of pregnancy, a wonderful way to wait for the child.

When Nicole actually decided to come forth into the world, the younger doctor was on call. He was also absolutely terrific, and funny, which added a nice note to the delivery room. As Nicole started to emerge, he asked, what names have you chosen? We told him what we'd picked for a boy, and a girl. And he said as he delivered her, "Iiiiii....ittttt's **Nicole**!"

I have never forgotten those moments, or many more from that time.

Our Own Kids

- Thinking back to the time pre-birth, what do you remember?
- Did your doctor discuss the miracle of birth, as I was lucky enough to have experienced?
- Did you have any information on what was happening month by month as you waited for the big day?
- If so, were these pictures?
- Whether or not you had this information, wasn't this about the most exciting thing you'd ever seen going on, and been a part of?
- Or were you feeling differently while waiting for your child to be born? Some people feel anxious and frightened, and a million other ways. What's the best way to describe how you felt while you were waiting, and then immediately upon the birth?

One of the things I remember is being filled with overwhelming feelings of sheer love unlike any I'd ever experienced, during the days after giving birth at Lying-In Hospital in New York. (In those days, women were allowed to rest up after birth for a few days, before going home. Quite civilized versus today.) The love continued, in a different form – taking care of the baby, Nicole, breast-feeding, bathing her, changing her – all of these reinforced the feelings of responsibility for a tiny being, but at the same time, they reinforced enormous emotional ties. Especially when that tiny being looked up at me, or grasped my finger, or any of those wonderful things babies do to be sure you will take care of them even when they make a mess in their diapers.

When our daughter reached the ripe old age of six months, she was clearly laughing. Of course the doctor thought I was crazy when I told him. But then I demonstrated. I did some thing or another that always got a reaction, and sure enough, Nicole laughed. The doctor had to admit it really happened, much to his surprise.

. . . .

There was also the moment when we introduced the cats to our daughter. We put Nicole in the middle of our queen size bed, and let the cats come up and sniff. We watched carefully – many people had told us cats hurt babies, and we were ready for a quick move if needed. But the cats never did a thing to harm her. I was reminded of how a cat we had when I was a kid reacted when my little brother hit him. He seemed to know this was a kid, and simply waited until he could get away. Never, ever did he hit back. Though he was fierce with any animal that tried to poach his turf.

- When your first child was born, what were you feeling? What was your spouse feeling?
- How did other family respond?

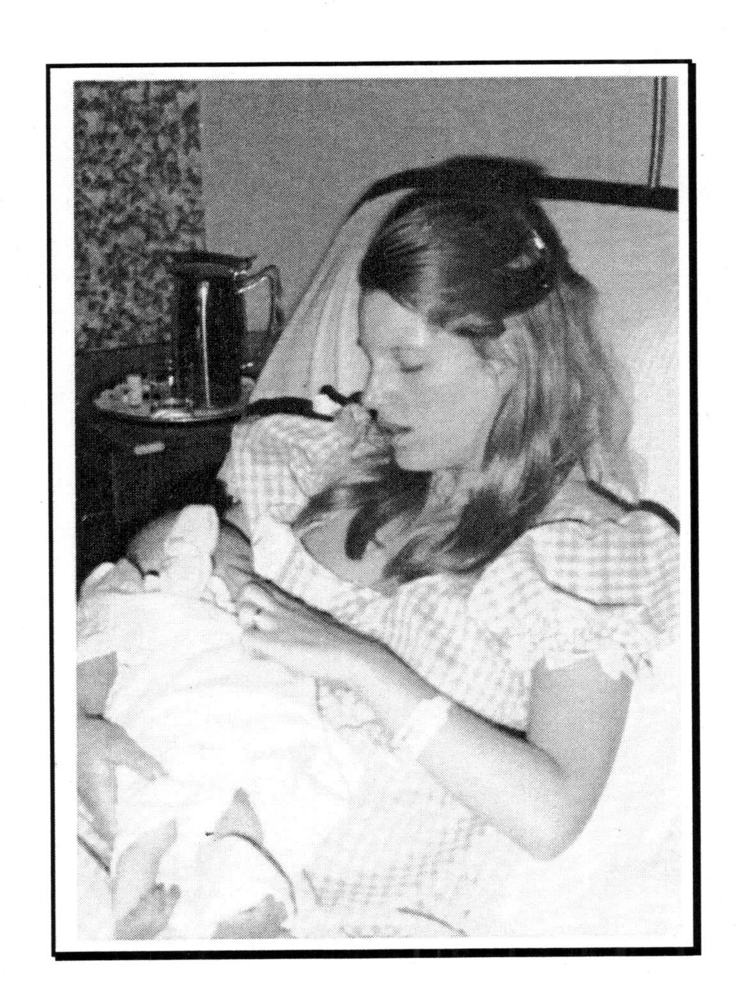

- Did you (did your wife) give birth at home? In a hospital?
- If a hospital, what was the trip like, getting there?
- What happened during labor? If you're a woman, did you yell at your husband?
- Once you got home with the baby, what do you remember as happening the first few days, if you can remember this?

- How about the first few months? What are some of the happiest moments during this time?

- What are some of the worst moments?

- For me, maybe the worst thing was the lack of sleep. It seemed we would never get a good night's rest ever again. Sound familiar? Or were you one of those rats who had a kid who slept through the night right away?

SEAN McNELIS
7TH GRADE SCIENCE
PERIOD 5
MAY 16, 2001

A SPECIAL PERSON

In 1992, my Grandpa died. He was the nicest person. The night before he died, he talked to every person in our family and gave us a hug. I felt that night that he was leaving a paw print on our hearts forever.

Note: This story is reprinted with permission from the author and his parents. It was written as part of the Pawprints Literacy Plus Educator Workshop training program conducted for the Jane Goodall Institute's Roots and Shoots program in Los Angeles. The teacher was Ginger Krell, from the Lone Hill Middle School, in San Dimas, CA.

- As the kid(s) were growing up, what are some of your fondest memories?
- When have you been proudest of your kids?
- Have you had wrangles with the kids? How did you all handle this?

Nicole Hillebrandt, age 3, performs at a dance recital. Seen here with her doting mom and dad after dashing across the stage in the surprise move she invented, and that her choreographer-teacher decided to leave in the piece.

I can remember very well how I got my first pet. I was six or seven years old, and we were living in Culver City, California. We had a house that is still there today. I drive by it from time to time on my way to visit a recently acquired friend who lives only three blocks away, and always marvel at how small the world is, in some ways.

But, I digress. To continue with the pet story...One day I was working on my own little pansy garden my Mom had helped me create, when a black and white kitten appeared. I called him, and he came right over. He let me pick him up, and started to purr. I noticed he had a clump of dirt in his fur. I ran inside with him, and said to my Mom, "Can we keep him? He must not have a home. Look. He has dirt in his fur!" My Mom said, "Ask your father." When my father came home from his "shop" that evening (he was an interior designer at the time), I repeated my request, being sure to include the note about the dirt. My Dad said, "Ask your mother." My parents finally had to talk to each other when I revealed that I'd already asked my Mom. They tried to find out if there were an owner, but none appeared. And so, I became the extremely happy friend of the cat who came to be known as Velvet, because once he got cleaned up, that's how his fur felt.

Pets

- When you were a kid, did you have a pet?
- What did you have?
- How did you get this pet?
- Did you have to bug your mother? Your father? Tell the story.
- Who took care of the pet?
    - Did you?
    - Your brother/sister(s)?
    - Your parents?
    - Did you get in trouble for not taking care of the pet when you were supposed to?

VELVET

By Ina Lee Silvert, age 7

Velvet is my cat,

Whom I dearly love to pat.

He is black and white,

And will not scratch or bite.

He likes to play with string,

And almost anything.

He's big, strong and fat.

He's Velvet, my cat.

- Can you remember a specific story about your first pet, something that was fun for you both?
- Do you remember teaching him/her any tricks?
- Or your pet teaching you tricks?
- What was the very best thing about having this pet?

SAVED BY A DUCK

By Eliza Crawford, August 8, 2003

When my child was three months old, my husband brought home a cute white duckling. After a few days he brought home a pedigreed police dog. He said he paid a big sum of money for the dog, and we should not let it loose.

My husband was a Police Chief. One morning he got an emergency call to come right in to work, and left the house early.

Now this dog was a one-man dog. So when she didn't see my husband, she started barking and running about. I ran to the baby and covered him with a blanket from top to toe. The duck ran under my son's bed, fluffed his feathers and lifted his feet in an attack position.

The dog came toward us, very furious. The room we were in had two doors. I opened one. Thank God the dog ran through it. I banged it shut. The dog barked and threw herself at the door. I didn't open it.

When the servant came, he shouted, "The dog has gone mad!" It was running wildly about. I threw the collar to the servant and asked him to collar the dog 'till my husband came home. Other people had refused to come near her.

I waited 'till my husband arrived and then I asked him to give away the dog, pedigreed or not, costly or not. And that is what we did, in the end.

Meanwhile, the duckling was calm and sat under my son's bed 'till my husband appeared. It was a small duckling, but there to protect my son, thank God.

Note: Author Eliza Crawford, also an alum of our Pawprints Writing Club in Los Angeles, lived in a British enclave in India for many years, where this story is set. You can find more of Eliza's stories on our website, http://www.InasPawprints.com, and in the new books, "Stories from the Heart," Vols. 1 and 2, through our site or Amazon.com.

- Did you get other pets? What kind? Did you have to bug your parents again?
- Were your pets indoor critters? Outdoor?
- What did they look like? Feel like? Sound like?
- Did other people like them?
- Did they get into trouble?
- What were some annoying traits your pets had?

HONKING FISH

RAPSCALLION P. CAT, a.k.a. "RAPPER"

I was sitting in the big claw foot tub, with the door open, alone in the apartment except for my kitten, Rapper. He was in the next room, and I happened to glance over at him. All of a sudden, he got into stalk position, tail swishing, eyes riveted on me. I ducked down inside the tub and waited a few seconds. When I popped my head up, Rapper had advanced several steps. He froze, front paw midair, when he saw me. I ducked again.

We kept this up for a few minutes until he arrived, jumped up and batted at me, carefully, claws retracted. Since I proved to be such a good student, he later taught me how to play fetch.

Of all the men long gone in my life, I think he's the one I miss the most.

- What were the most endearing traits?
- Do you have pets now? Do you think your experiences as a kid led to this?
- Did you let your kids have pets?

Travels

Just for a change of pace, here's a different way of jogging your memory:

- The very first trip I ever took I had a __________time!
- We went to _____________ and it was absolutely _____________!
- We were _________________________years old.
- I was alone/with ___________________________.
- I have /have not gone back, because ________________.

You might want to think of more trips and the sights you've enjoyed, both alone and with others. And places you would like to see that you've already seen, along with places you have never seen and would like to see now.

Travel gives us topics that are usually really fun for all of us, armchair travelers and those who like to get out there and go! And it's also a perfect setting for zillions of pictures.

Hobbies

- When I was a kid, I liked to ________________________.
- The most fun doing these things was __________________.
- Now that I am a grownup, I still like to______________________, when I have spare time.
- Even when I don't have spare time, it's important to me to _______________.
- I would/would not recommend hobbies to other people because _______________________.

Looking Back – Inventions....

- Think of some of the inventions you have born witness to over the course of your life.
  - What one stands out as really impressing you at the time it first came about?
  - Why were you impressed?
  - Were other people impressed?
  - What did this invention accomplish?
  - What did it replace?
  - Thinking back with the advantage of hindsight, was it a good idea this invention came to be?
  - What makes you say that?

- What other inventions come to mind?
    - Think about the first time you used one of these.
    - How did it feel?
    - Where were you?
    - What were you wearing?
    - What happened?
    - Were you excited?

- Think about how your life was changed by these inventions.

  - How were others' lives changed?
  - How was the country, and perhaps the world changed?
  - Are these changes good for people?
  - Bad? Why?
  - How about the planet?
  - How about animals?

- Think about telephones, air travel, television, radio, and now the computer.
  - Any special memories of early times for each of these inventions come up for you?
  - How do you think they affect the lives of people?

Looking Back – Times, Eras, Big Events

- Think back to various times in our country that you lived through, such as the Depression.
  - Can you think of some specific moments during those years that left a lasting impression on you?
  - Or some small event(s) that happened during that time?
  - Many of us have seen pictures of people lining up in bread lines, and of hobos riding the rails.
  - Did you or anyone you know ever personally see or experience any of these things?
  - What did you see?
  - How did you feel?
  - How did others involved feel?
  - What do you think it meant for the country?
  - Have you seen anything like it since?

- Think back to WWII.
  - Where were you?
  - Did you or members of your family fight in the War?
  - Where?
  - What changes happened in your family as a result of the war?
  - Do you remember anything you did during those years?
  - What your feelings were at the time?

Hearing possibly imaginary German voices, I managed to get past any snipers that I may have passed near. And then, I heard the sweetest words of my lifetime, 'Halt! Who goes they-ah?'

A tiny segment from many stories about events that took place during his time as a pilot during WWII, by Howard Westley, from "Halt! Who Goes They-ah?" in "Stories From The Heart," Vol. 2

- When WWII ended, where were you?
  - How did you hear?
  - What were your feelings?
  - Were you alone or with others?
  - What was going on around you?
  - Do you remember any specifics, colors, sounds, smells, happenings, interactions among people? (For a sample recollection, see page 18).

- Do you remember the first time man set foot on the moon?
- What were you feeling?
- Where were you?
- Who were you with?
- What was everyone wearing?
- What were people saying?
- Do you remember the name of the astronaut who first set his foot down on our heavenly companion?
- Do you remember his words?

- When you read "Sputnik," what comes to mind?

- When you read, “The Beatles,” what comes to mind?

- What does the name "Katherine Hepburn" suggest to you?

- How about Humphrey Bogart?

- List some of your favorite movie stars growing up. Write a little story retelling an incident about them you remember, or about a part they played in a movie.

Thinking Back over Personal Events in Your Own Life ...

- What one thing are you absolutely thrilled happened, and would never want any different?

- What goals are you pleased you reached? Or did you somehow sort of just get to where you are? And what are the best things about where you are right now?

- If there were one thing you could do differently, what would that be? Why? What would happen?

- If you could go back to any particular time, what would that be?
  - Where would you be?
  - What would you be doing?
  - Wearing?
  - Hearing, seeing, smelling?
  - How would you be feeling?
  - What would be the best part about being there?

- If you could have avoided one thing that happened in your life, what would that be?
  - Why?

- Have you lost people in your life? (Start with any you feel comfortable thinking about, move on to others if and when you like.)

  - Family?
  - Friends?
  - What are your memories of those people?
  - What do you miss the most about this person?
  - What memory do you treasure most?

- Imagine that person were in the room right now. What would he or she say to you?

- Thinking about younger people today, what do you think is important for them to know?

  - What would you advise kids?
  - Parents?
  - Young adults?

Notes

Pawpress Product and Order Form

We have a collection of items that you might find useful – and fun – to help you with your project. There are also goodies that make purr-fect gifts for kids and grownups in our "In Paws We Trust" and "May the Paws be with you" lines. Here is a sampling. For more items, please visit our website, http://www.InasPawprints.com and our online store at http://www.cafepress.com/PawprintsShop. Or drop us a line and we'll send you the full catalog. Order info and form on the next page.

As seen on TV

Pawprints, © 1999 Ina Hillebrandt
The amazon.com best selling book of Short "tails" to aMUSE Kids and Adults.
Item B1

"In Paws We Trust" tote featuring Rapper P. Cat in his garden. Handsome Doggie bag, too.
Item F3

"In Paws We Trust" mug, shown with Rapper. Handsome Dog also available. Both are *Pawprints* stars.
Item F1

"In Paws We Trust" Teddy for Cat-Loving Kids. Dog lover version, too. *Item F2*

New!

Stories From The Heart Vol. 1
Fanciful and true tales by seniors. Compiled, Edited and designed by Ina Hillebrandt
© 2004
Item B2

Amazon.com Bestseller

Stories From The Heart Vol. 2 – From great grape fiascos to wars… wit and wisdom from a range of continents, countries and times. Compiled, Edited and designed by Ina Hillebrandt
© 2005
Item B5

"May the Paws Be With You" Mousepad designed by Handsome, Star of *Pawprints. Rapper Super MouserPad* also available
Item F4

Official Pawprints Journal. Record your Feelings, Thoughts, Memories, Funny Moments, Bugging Moments, Dreams. Featuring Rapper P. Cat. Also available with Handsome Dog cover for dog people. 160 pages.
Item B3

New!

How to Write Your Memoirs © 2004 makes it easy and fun to create a marvelous present for your family
Item B4

"In Paws We Trust" Baseball jersey featuring Handsome. Available with Rapper, too!
Item F5

NOTE: Please retain a copy of the filled-in form for your records. Mail with check payable to: "Ina Hillebrandt/ Pawpress." Address: Pawpress, PO Box 492213, Los Angeles, CA 90049. We accept Visa and Master Card. Your statement will show payment to SEE/Pawprints Literacy Plus Foundation. If paying by card, you can also fax us your order: 310-471-7528.

Name as it appears on card: ______________________________ Card # ______________________________

Expiration Date ___________ Amt. ______________ Your signature ______________________________

Billing address: ________________________ City ______________ State _____ Zip _________ Country ______

Shipping address (if different from billing address): Recipient's Name ______________________________

Recipient's address ____

Is this a gift? If so, we will include a card for you! Yes ___No ___ Orders are filled and shipped within one week of receipt. Please allow two weeks by mail, 7 days by fax. Expedited 2-day shipping available. Add $10.

PAWPRESS ORDER FORM

Code	Description	Price	Quantity	Total
B1	***Pawprints***, by Ina ISBN 1880882-01-9 *Available also through amazon.com and bookstores*	$12.95		
B2	***Stories from the Heart*** ISBN 1880882-04-3 Memoirs Fanciful and True by Seniors *Available online through our website and amazon.com*	$19.95		
B3	***Official Pawprints Journal*** featuring Handsome, World's Best Dog, from *Pawprints* ISBN 1880882-05-1	$10.95		
B3B	***Official Pawprints Journal*** for Cat People, featuring Rapper P. Cat, *from Pawprints* ISBN 1880882-06-X (not shown)	$10.95		
B4	***How to Write Your Memoirs –*** *makes writing, and reading – your life stories a pleasure! Available online through our website and amazon.com*	$24.95		
B5	***Stories From The Heart, Vol. 2*** From great grape fiascos to wars, wit an wisdom from a range of continents, countries and times ISBN 1-800882-08-6 *Available online through our website and amazon.com*	$19.95		
F1	**"In Paws We Trust" large mug**, with Rapper, *Pawprints star*	$15.99		
F1B	**"In Paws We Trust" large mug,** with Handsome (not shown)	$15.99		
F2	"In Paws We Trust" **Teddy Bear** for Cat-Loving Kids	$16.99		
F2B	**Teddy Bear** for Dog-Lovers featuring Handsome (not shown)	$16.99		
F3	"In Paws We Trust" **tote bag** featuring Rapper P. Cat in his garden	$16.99		
F4	**Mousepad** designed by Handsome, Star of *Pawprints.*	$14.99		
F4B	*Rapper* **mousepad** *features the picture as shown on the tote bag* (not shown)	$14.99		
F5	"In Paws We Trust" **Baseball jersey** featuring Handsome.	$20.99		
F5B	**Baseball jersey** with Rapper as shown on tote (not shown)	$20.99		
Sub-total				
Tax – California shipments: please add 8.25 % sales tax				
Shipping and handling: Please add $4.95 for orders $12.95 or under. For orders $12.95 - $24.95, please add $7.50. For orders $25 +, please add $1.05 per item to base s/h price of $7.50.				
TOTAL				

Notes

Would you like help in getting your own memoirs into book form, for your family and friends, or perhaps a larger audience?

We are very proud to announce that *Stories From The Heart, Vol. 2* – the new collection of memoirs from the Pawprints Writing Club designed and published by Pawpress – has made the Amazon.com bestseller list. You will find some excerpts in this book and on our website at InasPawprints.com

Or would you be interested in a Memoir Writing Class yourself?

Read what some of our "Stories From The Heart" writers have to say:

"Makes my week!"

"Expands my mind."

"Opened the floodgates."

"Enlivening, spirited discussions in writings."

"Interesting and inspirational."

"Wonderfully uplifting."

"Unlocked the doors to memories long forgotten but still present."

"The participants are nice, the group inclusive; I've made a lot of new friends."

"It's just plain fun!"

Contact Ina to find out how to set up a
Pawprints Writing Club for your group
– or –
For information on how to get help with creating
or publishing a finished book of your own.

http://www.InasPawprints.com
E-mail: Inah@InasPawprints.com
Telephone: 310.471.5048